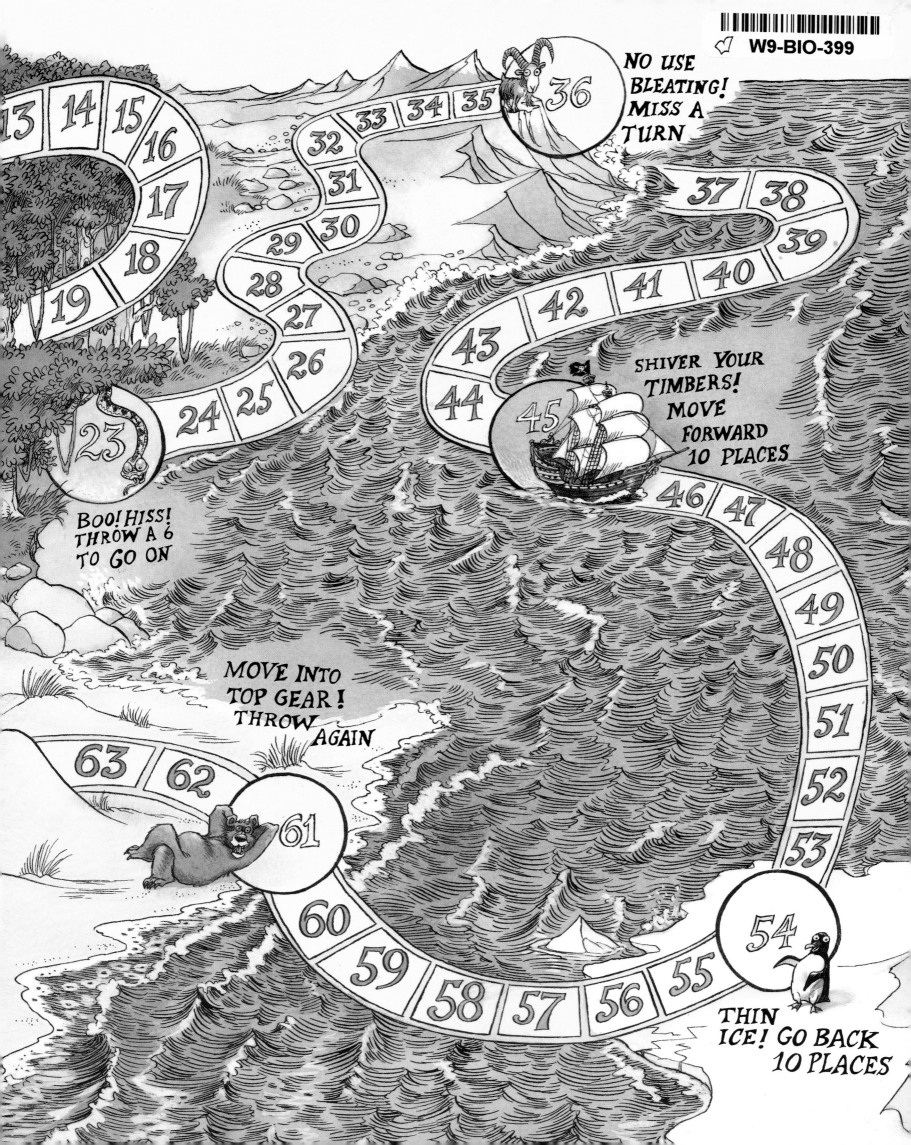

SIMON & SCHUSTER BOOKS FOR YOUNG READERS
Simon & Schuster Building, Rockefeller Center
1230 Avenue of the Americas, New York, New York, 10020
Text copyright © 1991 by Kathryn Cave
Illustrations copyright © 1991 by Chris Riddell
First published by Frances Lincoln Limited, Great Britain
First U.S. edition 1992
All rights reserved including the right of reproduction
in whole or in part in any form.
SIMON & SCHUSTER BOOKS FOR YOUNG READERS
is a trademark of Simon & Schuster.
Manufactured in Hong Kong

10 9 8 7 6 5 4 3 2 1

Library of Congress Cataloging-in-Publication Data
Cave, Kathyrn.   Out For the Count/by Kathryn Cave;
illustrated by Chris Riddell. Summary: On a night
that he can't sleep, Tom begins to count sheep
who promptly go to sleep on his bedroom floor except
for one that leads him on a variety of numerical
adventures.   [1. Stories in rhyme.   2. Counting.
3. Bedtime—Fiction.   4. Animals—Fiction.]
I. Riddell, Chris, ill.   II. Title.   PZ8.3.C317Tr
1992   [E]—dc20   91-22096
ISBN 0-671-75591-9

OUT FOR THE COUNT

A COUNTING ADVENTURE

by KATHRYN CAVE

illustrated by CHRIS RIDDELL

SIMON & SCHUSTER BOOKS FOR YOUNG READERS
Published by Simon & Schuster
New York · London · Toronto · Sydney · Tokyo · Singapore

One night Tom couldn't sleep. He'd had
three drinks of water from his dad,
six hugs and four good-nights from Mom;
but even so, sleep wouldn't come.
At 10 o'clock his dad said, "Right.
This is your very last good-night.
I'm off to bed. Now go to sleep—
and if you can't, try counting sheep."

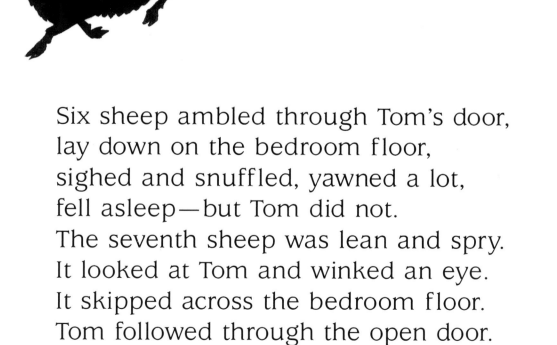

Six sheep ambled through Tom's door,
lay down on the bedroom floor,
sighed and snuffled, yawned a lot,
fell asleep—but Tom did not.
The seventh sheep was lean and spry.
It looked at Tom and winked an eye.
It skipped across the bedroom floor.
Tom followed through the open door.

Through the doorway lay a wood,
wild and fearsome. There Tom stood
wondering—until a growl
warned him wolves were on the prowl.
Two wolves, four wolves, six, eight, ten.
Soon Tom had counted twelve. And then,
because there was no place to flee,
Tom thought it best to climb a tree.

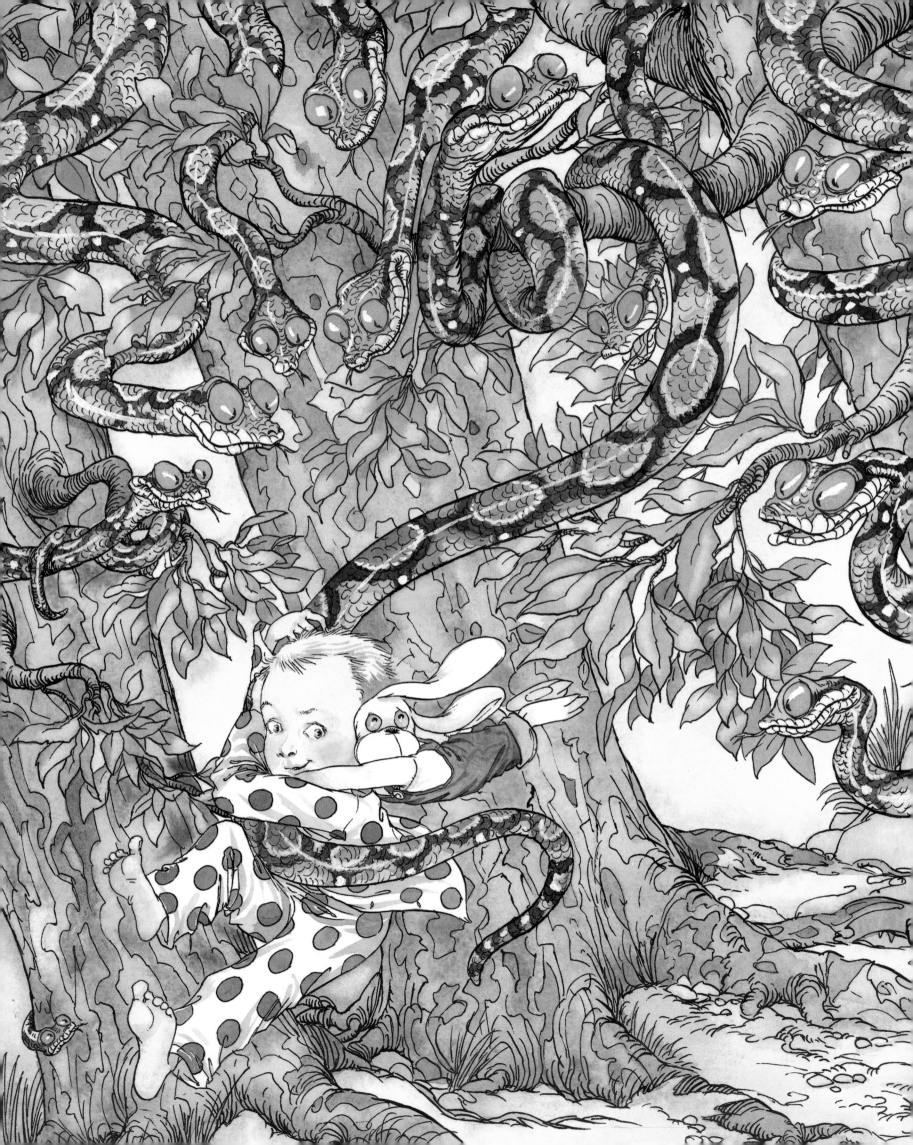

There's no place safer than up high
unless a python happens by,
for pythons rarely knock or phone
and they don't visit you alone.
Tom counted 23, and so
he certainly was smart to go.

The mountainside was cold and bare.
The wind that whistled through Tom's hair
brought to his ears a plaintive note:
the mournful bleating of a goat.
Some goats are small, some goats are sweet.
Not Tom's—they had big horns and feet.
And when the 36 played rough,
Tom couldn't exit fast enough.

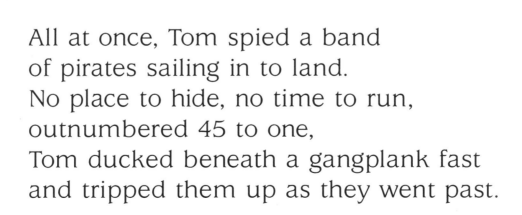

All at once, Tom spied a band
of pirates sailing in to land.
No place to hide, no time to run,
outnumbered 45 to one,
Tom ducked beneath a gangplank fast
and tripped them up as they went past.

Suddenly the wind grew colder.
Penguins crowded round Tom's shoulder,
30, 40, 54,
all the penguins on the shore.
When Tom had counted every one
he paddled off in search of sun.

The beach looked like the perfect spot
for Tom to sunbathe. It was not,
for 61 enormous bears
all seemed to think that it was theirs.
Perhaps they only meant to play,
but Tom was glad to drive away.

I like a car that's bright and new,
that goes just where you want it to
and does not stop in eerie places,
where the bats have hungry faces.
One vampire bat's enough for me.
If you bump into 70,
don't stay to count them—call your mom
and head for shelter fast, like Tom.

Ghosts are fine in ones or twos,
depending on the sort you choose.
On gloomy Sundays when it's raining,
some can be quite entertaining.
But 88 gave Tom a fright
and so he simply said
goodnight.

Bengal tigers can be kind.
All the same, if you should find
97 in a heap,
the best thing is to let them sleep.
Tom tiptoed past and took great care
not to tweak a single hair.

A hundred shadows big and small
beckoned from Tom's bedroom wall.
He shut the door, tucked in the sheep,
put out the light and went to sleep.